Women! Get The Material Things You Really Want From Men

A straight forward guide for women who are fed up with seeking love and relationships

Dema Shamel

iUniverse, Inc.
New York   Bloomington

iUniverse books may be ordered through booksellers or by contacting:

iUniverse
1663 Liberty Drive
Bloomington, IN 47403
www.iuniverse.com
1-800-Authors (1-800-288-4677)

http://www.getwhatyouwantnow.net

ISBN: 978-1-4401-6688-4 (sc)
ISBN: 978-1-4401-6689-1 (ebook)

Printed in the United States of America

iUniverse rev. date: 02/01/2010

Introduction

Let's face it: women are conditioned to be emotional creatures who believe in love and the picket fence that goes with it. Men have been playing women and getting what they want from them since the beginning of time. This book was written to teach women the skills and techniques in a formulaic, businesslike way to bring maximum happiness and, perhaps more importantly, money or material objects that they want from men.

Working as an exotic dancer and applying everything I've learned from that experience to my daily life has granted me many wishes. The most important thing that I learned from being in an environment where money is exchanged for a cheap thrill is that in actuality power was being exchanged for power.

This is not a book about finding love, but if that's what you want, you might be able to use ideas from this book to get a man to fall in love with you. This book describes an unconventional way to get what you want from men. Enjoy!

Dedication

I dedicate this book to my mom. Watching her in her relationships with men allowed me to learn about what I want and do not want in mine. I also dedicate this book to my grandma, for having a big heart and undying love for her children. She has sacrificed so much of her life by raising her children and grandchildren. To my little brother, Dude, for being there when all we had was each other. To one of my best girlfriends, Tashima, for being there from the beginning of our female development and relationships.

Also, to my dad, thank you for the Twix candy bars that made me smile; you always did have the nice-guy approach, and because of you, that's the kind of guy I became drawn to. Good guys can finish first if they know how to give a girl what she wants. To my ex-husband, for giving me pain when I thought having a guy in the palm of my hand was pleasure; you sure know how to make a woman open her eyes without having a bitter taste in her mouth. I love all of you.

Chapter One

Know Yourself

If you don't know yourself, who does? What makes you happy? Draw a vertical line down the center of a piece of paper. Write on the left side of the line what makes you happy, and write what makes you sad on the right side of the page.

Of course, your list might be broad, so circle the things that affect you personally and are dear to you. I know you might want to solve world hunger, but does that affect you in your everyday life?

Now cross out the things that you wrote down on both lists that you have no control over. For example, you have no control over the size of your feet (unless you are interested in the ancient Chinese method of binding them). Once you have an idea of who you are, you will have a better chance of finding out what you want.

The list of your "happies" and "saddies" might become longer or shorter over time, so you might want to refer back to it periodically, or do this exercise twice a year for inventory purposes if the list is too long. If your list is too short, you might give it further thought for a couple of days before you move forward.

What is your personality like? Some people are really outgoing or shy or have a combination of different personality traits. You'll find that if you are really outgoing, you might be attracted to someone less outgoing than you.

When evaluating men, you should focus more on their personalities rather than on their physical appearance. If you develop feelings for a man, you will likely find him more handsome. You know the old saying, "Love is blind"? There is truth to that, but trust me, you don't want to be a blind fool. I am not saying that you should go out and find a great guy who is unattractive; why not find a great guy with a personality that fits well with most of the things that make you happy?

When meeting a man, ask questions and talk about things that you wrote down on your happy and sad list (do not tell him about this list). His responses to your questions will help you decide if he is a keeper or not. If you find yourself checking off more things from your sad list during a conversation with a guy, then he's probably not the one you're looking for.

For example, if you have nothing in common with a guy, he should be relegated to your sad list, but if he is in sync with most of your opinions and beliefs, he should be considered a compatible guy and placed on your happy list. The happy-list guy is a keeper, and the sad-list guy is a waste of your time.

When creating this list, remember to be specific, but be careful not to overdo it. Keep the list direct, and do not create or imagine things that might make you happy or sad. Only write what you are certain of, and be honest with yourself.

While you will go by their responses and your instincts to help you find a man, there is truly no way to cookie cut it. You must get a feel for a guy to see if he responds to the things that make you happy or sad. If he feels the same way as you do about the things that make you happy and sad, then he might be the guy to give you what you want. You are merely looking at a general blueprint of these guys that will help you with your final determination of where they fall on your list.

Don't forget that he will be checking you out as well. Men look for and admire certain qualities and personality traits in women. By possessing these qualities and personality traits, you might have a greater chance of getting what you want more quickly, because these qualities fascinate and intrigue men. These are some attributes that men usually find attractive in women:

Energy—Men love women with good vibes and lots of energy. If a man compliments you on your energy, you are doing something right. It's very common for a guy to say, "You have nice eyes," and "I love your lips," but he is paying close attention to your personality if he says he likes your energy and compliments you on it rather than just complimenting your physical appearance.

Sexiness—Women can be sexy in many ways. Men might find women sexy in anything from a hot nightgown to a tank top and boy shorts, but real sexiness comes from within. A woman can be in her late 60s and still be sexy as hell. It's not all about age.

Easygoing attitude—A man will run to a woman who is calm and cool and not naggy or bitchy. He will think of her when he needs a friend or someone to confide in. Do not think this woman is gullible or naïve; this one usually has a plan and knows what she is doing.

Intelligence—A woman doesn't have to be a rocket scientist to attract a man, but she needs to think fast and be able to speak on just about any subject ranging from world news to pop culture. This lady is very knowledgeable and sharp and will teach you a thing or too. She will invest at least a few hours a week in reading and learning what is going on in the world.

Warning! This is not about how many degrees a woman possesses or her level of education. Do not bore a man with stories about you, you, you, and your degrees. He is interested in your personality and his physical attraction to you. Also, if it applies, let this person know that you are interested in some kind of business, education, etc. Most businessmen will be impressed and might offer you some insight and maybe mentor you or refer someone to help you. He might want to take you under his wing.

Gratitude—Always say please and thank you. It's a no-brainer, but believe it or not, some women do not say it. Make politeness a way of life. Men already like to feel needed. Allow him to feel appreciated.

Confidence—This probably should be at the top of the list. There is nothing more powerful than a woman who is naturally comfortable in her skin. You don't have to be high maintenance or be constantly looking in the mirror. This woman just knows she has it together. It's in her walk, talk, and attitude.

Submissiveness—No, this doesn't refer to S&M, this is about letting a man feel like a man. Let him feel like he is the big guy every now and then, and I am sure you'll be rewarded. Independent women get so caught up in doing things for themselves, that a lot of times they forget that they are ladies first and will resist when a man just wants to open the door for them.

Humor—Laughter is the key to everyone's soul, including a man's. Being funny means being sexy and clever and not necessarily a stand-up comedian. A woman should be playful and flirty and have a funny story or two that's not too "I'm hanging out with the boys"-ish. For example, if a guy compliments how beautiful you are, sexy/playfully say, "I know." He'll light up, but be ready for a sexy and flirty comeback, and always end the exchange by letting him know that you're joking and appreciate the compliment.

Decisiveness—If a man gives you an opportunity to tell him what you want, do not pass it up due to indecisiveness. If you are a smart woman, you should know that a lot of quality men are businessmen, and if you don't seal the deal, another dealmaker will.

Practice saying in your head or write down on paper what you want from men. Prepare yourself for any question you think you might hear from any of them. Make sure you know what you want for your birthday, Christmas, where you want to travel, what are your favorite restaurants, (all the questions guys ask or you wish they would ask). Just be prepared, or you might lose your opportunity to tell him again.

Independence—Never appear to be too available, needy, or clingy. It's a definite turn off. Act as though you need to pencil him in or check your schedule without sounding like a complicated prude who is way too busy for him. Have hobbies and spend time with family and friends, and of course, other guys. It's OK to create illusions; just make sure they aren't too farfetched.

Refrain from appearing desperate, and remember that if you put all your eggs in one basket, you might become emotionally attached. You should focus on your own personal life goals and dreams. Protect yourself so that you only give 80% of yourself and save 20% to insure your sanity.

Spending most of your time dating one guy might make you feel emotionally attached, and it can get ugly, ladies. I feel pretty confident that most women have been there at least once. Why would you want to go back there again? Getting what you want from men is not about you being emotionally attached to them.

Patience—Although men are really persistent and might try faster than you can say the word "sex" to have sex with you, they will respect you more in the long run if you don't submit to them right away. Keep in mind that you want to keep this guy around for the long haul, so be smart and dangle your jewel like it is candy in front of a baby. Remember to always be responsible for your actions, don't take yourself too seriously, and have fun. Imagine yourself as a sexy, fearless, spontaneous, mysterious, and interesting woman that all men desire.

If you don't believe it, who will? Feel sexy and walk around town and watch the reactions of men around you. Hell, watch the reactions of women, too. If you are seriously feeling sexy, you will exude it, and people will notice.

Take a moment and think about sucking a lemon. Do you start to feel your mouth water because you know the familiar, sour taste of a lemon? When you think of going on a sunny, relaxing vacation, do you already see the sandy beaches? You want to be thought of as a wonderful vacation, not as a sour lemon.

What do you think are your best assets? If you aren't working them, you need to start today. If friends or strangers compliment your legs, helloooo, show off those legs. Wear the minis, stretch pants, and jeans to show off and accent your shape. Every woman possesses beauty, no matter what God gave her. She just has to know what that is and work it.

If you have hang-ups, get over them. We already crossed out the things we have no control over, so cross them out of your thoughts. If you need to lose weight, what are you waiting for? Nurture your body with exercise. Release tension while sculpting your muscles. You can do a variety of exercises, from Pilates to weight training, and most importantly, cardio. Save money by purchasing workout videos and exercising at home.

Local recreational centers might have low-cost memberships that allow you access to workout equipment. When you exercise regularly and watch what you eat, you'll look and feel great. You'll release endorphins, and if you know anything about endorphins, you know about releasing happy juice. It relieves stress, gives us energy, (for guys to compliment) and along with a healthy diet, it creates wellness.

Diets are interesting. I will not go on and on about which ones to try, but I will suggest that you stay away from the trendy ones. Most of us can control our eating habits and physical activity to achieve our fitness goals. Visit mypyramid.org or speak to a nutritionist for more information on nutrition.

Once you have control over your life, stay clear of the things that make you sad and look toward the things that make you happy. I don't know about you, but I would rather be walking around with a smile on my face than a frown any day. In order for someone to think you are great, you have to think it first, and you have to mean it. Don't get caught up in false feelings and negative thoughts about yourself.

You deserve something wonderful, and a lot of women allow men to treat them poorly instead of like the jewels that they are, because of negative feelings, negative self-image, self-esteem issues, and insecurities. Please do not allow magazines and other air-brushed delusions to negatively affect your thoughts about self-love and beauty.

When you don't believe you are a star, you can find yourself in unhealthy relationships, battling promiscuity, settling for what you don't want, and being unhappy. You can have all the money in the world, or be with a guy who has all the money in the world, but if you aren't at peace with yourself, you could be one of the unhappiest people in the world.

Look in the mirror and tell yourself that you love yourself. Repeat some positive affirmations and mean them. This will boost your self-esteem, even if you possess a lot of it already. This book is about how to get what you want from men, but everything begins with you, so right now you need to concentrate on getting what you want from yourself, and that's the start of a positive outlook.

Have a spiritual routine or ritual. Whatever keeps you centered, practice it. Center yourself, and develop a spiritual routine so that you will harmoniously have balance and stability. If you do not have a healthy spiritual regimen, you might find yourself feeling all over the place, inconsistent, and/or unbalanced. When you're unbalanced, you appear to be a little wishy-washy, and that's not healthy.

You should be an emotionally, spiritually stable woman on the right track to healthiness. You should know who you are, you should love yourself, and you should be confident in yourself. This is the beginning of developing your new way of life. Set spiritual goals and live up to them. If you are involved in spirituality already, good for you. You are one step closer to knowing who you are. If you are slacking and haven't focused on spirituality in a while, pick it back up. It's harder than it sounds, but have faith in yourself. You can do it.

The way you carry yourself affects the kind of men you attract, with a few exceptions. In order to keep them interested, you should appear to have yourself together, or they will not be all that into you once they find out that you aren't stable. If you want to attract quality, you must possess it.

Review the happy and sad list you completed at the beginning of this chapter, and refer to it if you feel a little unsure about yourself. Feel free to read this chapter again if you need more motivation. Once you identify the areas where you need improvement, fix them right away and don't procrastinate.

The happies and saddies exercise is intended to make you to think about what you want and enjoy in life. Do not make a long list of things that you look for in a man. Men that you meet and date must qualify for your happy list and should be eliminated if they have more in common with your sad list. When meeting and dating men, the goal is to assess their personality traits and to make sure that they share some of the same interests that you have on your happies list and to eliminate anyone who has too much in common with your sad list.

Get rid of all baggage and put away any negative past experiences. Know your worth, concentrate on the things that matter, and start taking control of your life by knowing and loving yourself. Once you start that process, you will develop confidence from within. You will have emotional stability, and people around you will notice a positive change in your behavior. Trust yourself when making these adjustments. You must believe that you are special and beautiful, no matter what.

Take a look at the traits that turn men on, and look inside and think about what traits you have. Pretending to be someone you aren't isn't the way to go. You don't have to have all of these traits, but I guarantee that if you possess at least two of them, you will be okay.

How do you look? Let's take a look at the way you wear your hair. Maybe it's time for a new 'do. You can go to your local beauty school if you are on a tight budget and can't afford salon prices. Some of these students are very good at styling hair and are monitored by instructors. Check out hairstyle magazines or ask the stylist what he or she thinks would work for you if you can't decide. If you see a stylist doing a great job while you are waiting, ask him or her to do your hair. When you are out and you see a woman or girl with a great look, ask her who did her hair.

Make an appointment for a free makeup consultation and ask the makeup artist how to highlight your features in ways you might have never tried or might have forgotten. You don't have to be Tammy Faye Bakker, but a little makeup can enhance your natural beauty.

What's in your closet? Is it time to update your wardrobe for a new, sexy style that compliments your figure and your new attitude? A lot of style magazines have tips on affordable clothing styles and what works for your body type or size. Ask a sales associate at the clothing store for help, and remember: if you don't love it, don't buy it.

Once you know what to wear in public, it's time to discuss what you wear in private. Your lingerie should be sexy, feminine, new, and of good quality. Once your lingerie looks worn, discard it immediately. It does not matter if your old, worn-out piece of lingerie is your all-time favorite, do not keep it around for a rainy day. Never wear it again, period. This goes for your public clothing as well. Always look fresh and look your best, even when you are wearing your sporty style.

Positive affirmations to repeat:

Never say never or always.

You aren't too old for change or hope.

You are beautiful.

Chapter Two

What Do You Want?

You are fabulous, with great style and confidence, but do you have a clue about what you are looking for in a man?

Most women want an attractive man who is romantic, fun, and financially stable. Sounds pretty typical, doesn't it? But then women start to add to the list as they customize their dreamboat. Now he must have a college degree, a good relationship with his mother, be sensitive, and so on. There is nothing wrong with any of that, but is that what you really want?

In conventional dating, you meet a guy, you date, you like each other, then you date some more. If you love each other, maybe you get married. Case 1: You are happy and you have kids and grow old together, till death do you part. Case 2: After a while, you get bored, he gets bored, and you miss the good old days of courtship. Case 3: You should have just dated him and gotten what you wanted without all the strains and headache of a full-blown relationship.

Just because you love someone or like what he does for you, it doesn't mean you have to automatically entertain thoughts of marriage. Maybe you just want some of the benefits of a relationship without marriage. Do not base your decision to marry on love alone; look at it like a business plan or an executive decision.

For example, you might want a man for many different reasons, such as for a handyman around the house, or to help you out on bills or to buy you nice things, etc. It doesn't always have to lead to a committed relationship or marriage.

As we all know, divorce, separation, and break-ups can be devastating, and a lot of times we set ourselves up by thinking we have a "relationship" with a man. We do have to face that as women, we still have needs, desires, and wants from men. Make sure you can differentiate what your needs and wants are from each individual guy you are spending your time with.

Today, you are fancy and free. Guys are interested in you, and you might be interested in entertaining a dinner chat with one of these guys. You must first start off by asking the right questions in order to begin the process of elimination to find out if he fits in with more of your happies and less of your saddies.

Don't practice a script or interrogate your date. Casually and consciously ask him about his interests, and then pause and tell him about yours. He will think you are making small talk, but make sure you have your happies in mind, so the conversation flows smoothly. Also, take into consideration personality types; if he is quiet and shy, he might be drawn to more outgoing, free-spirited women.

If you find that your chat isn't going well, politely walk away from the situation. You will become more creative with practice. As you gain experience from sorting

these guys out, you will find that some of them can conform to what you want. You must be very selective, because this process can be time consuming, and you only want to spend time on men who are truly worth it.

Now, on the other hand, if everything is checking out fine, and the guy is looking and sounding great, how should you proceed? This will vary from man to man. Listen to your prospect closely. His speaking style is the key. If he says, for example, "Hello, madam, how are you?" respond in the same manner and tone by saying something like, "Fine, thank you, sir." If he says, "What's up?", you should say something like, "Nothing much, what's up with you?". These are just a few examples of speaking to a guy in the same style that he speaks to you. By mirroring the tone he uses, you create a comfort level with these guys. Make slight adjustments as needed, and always remember to be yourself.

Although men are sometimes similar to one another in their behavior, they are all somewhat different. What you might seek in one, you might not seek in another. Make eye contact, and remember to smile and have fun with these guys. Make them feel like the best place to be in the world is right there with you. Feel and be sexy, confident, smart, fun, funny, and flirty, but do not overdo it.

Do not talk too much about your past relationships. Keep your answers brief; your focus should be on the here and now and on qualifying this guy. Do not ask about any women in his life. You want him to focus on you. In a later chapter, what questions to ask about a previous relationship will be discussed, Keep this meeting casual, show interest in him, and be classy at all times. Have a diverse style, so that every time he sees you, he is secretly or openly excited about what you will be wearing and what will happen next.

Let him know that you like for your guy to spoil you and how you enjoy spoiling him, if that's what you want. When talking about how you like to spoil your guy, tell him something visually stimulating that's sexy, but stay away from raunchy. Keep it PG-13. Think bikini back rub, not nude massage. Tell him what you want without being too wordy, forward, pushy, or abrupt. Read his body language afterward.

Loyalty, money, and love are among the top few things that women want from men, but why? If you aren't looking for marriage or love, why would his loyalty matter so much to you, and who cares if he doesn't love you if you only want him to care for your needs? It is a well-known fact that most women love to shop, and in order to shop, it's nice to have men to give us money and buy things for us (even if we have our own). Gifts and surprises are nice, and men will give them to you if they like you or want to have sex with you. They do not have to necessarily love you.

Be selective with guys. Some of them are really deceptive, and if you smell bullshit, get out immediately. There was a time when guys had to spend a lot of money to look good, but not anymore. For the purposes of this book, an imposter is a guy who is not worthy of your time, because he is either cheap, is only out for sex, or is only concerned with his needs. You'll start to notice this imposter a mile away.

After being fooled a few times, your radar should go off when you encounter his type.

An imposters might act like he is "the man" at nightspots, hanging out with the guy in the VIP area who is actually buying the champagne, while the imposter is freeloading. Surprisingly, a small percentage of these scrub imposters actually do have money, but they are only interested in flossing it, not in spending it on you.

I've noticed that the wealthiest men tend to be some of the tightest ones, and the ones who make less money are sometimes the most generous.

Avoid the following:

1) Celebrities, entertainers, professional athletes, etc. These guys are the worst when it comes to getting what you want.

They have the whole world at their feet, and they know it so well. Women are giving them sex and whatever else they want, left and right. It is a fantasy of mine to marry a sexy footballer, but in reality, I know the chances are that I am just as likely to win the lottery. Very few women are successful with these men. Most of the time, these women are in the public eye, or they are someone the celebrity knew before they were famous, or they are that very lucky one-in-a-million girl who randomly met the celebrity and things worked out..

2) Clingy married men. These guys are the worst. They want you to be available whenever they are free, and they will make your head hurt as if you were the wife. Dump these guys the instant they are more trouble than they're worth. If you give them a second chance, they will continuously give you unnecessary grief again and again. If you can't handle getting what you don't want surpassing getting what you do want, do yourself a favor and let this one go.

3) Younger men. As women, we mature faster than men, and if they are a lot younger than we are, they tend to be arrogant and inexperienced. There might be a few exceptions out there, but I wouldn't waste my time on a much younger man. Find a mature man who has some life experience and financial achievements.

4) Jealous men. You do not need this in your life at all. Maybe in the beginning, it's cute, but life is short, and we have so many things in life we have to worry about and deal with that this issue shouldn't be one of them. These guys

can become verbally and physically abusive, so beware!

5) The roommate. If a guy is still doing the roommate thing or living with anyone who is not his wife or girlfriend, do not waste your time. If this guy is going through tough times, you are wasting your time, and you definitely do not want a Peter Pan frat boy. You want someone who is independent and financially together.

6) The dictator. This guy wants to tell you what to do and wants to watch over you like a micromanager. He wants to call all the shots. Don't mistake this for him being concerned. You'll find yourself giving up your own personal experiences in no time.

7) The smooth operator or player. He will make you weak in the knees, and you'll never know what happened. He is playing with a few girls and is always on the prowl.

8) The Know-it-all. He knows too much for his own good. If he is really all that intelligent, why does he need to brag? He can be full of sarcasm, be very condescending, and sharp-witted.

9) The super male model. If he looks prettier than you do and cares about looking in the mirror more than you do, you have a problem. You want to be the prettiest and most fashionable one in the relationship. Beware! this guy might not be a heterosexual man.

10) The cheapskate This guy is the opposite of what you're looking for. You want a gentleman who will spend money on you, not a cheapskate who wants to go Dutch on dinner.

Overall, you want to avoid any guy who doesn't offer you anything good. You are on a mission, and (although there are exceptions) if any of the guys you just read about get in your way, you will not get what you want.

Where do you meet the right guys? You can meet men everywhere you go, but they do not walk around with an "I spoil women" sign on their foreheads, so you have to dig through some debris to get to the right guy. You will begin by changing the way you think and adjusting your routines and activities. When you go shopping for groceries, to grab a coffee, or to have lunch, you will go to the more expensive neighborhoods. If you can afford it, start taking golf or tennis lessons. The whole idea is to go where the money is. Create a list of high-end places that you can include in your everyday routines.

Here are a few places or opportunities to consider when you are out prospecting men:

Happy hours. Try an expensive hotel; even if you do not drink, you can order a water or coffee. Do not stay longer than an hour if no one approaches you. Do not go to the same hotel more than once a month. Meet a friend there and arrive about fifteen minutes early. Check out the hotel's upcoming events and do a crash-bash attendance about an hour after the event starts. By that time, the ticket takers or head counters should be gone.

Charity events. Find out how to volunteer for big charity events or fundraisers in your area. You can help a great cause while prospecting at the same time. Volunteer for animal rescues and the Red Cross, and you will meet guys who are probably not shallow or self-absorbed. . Try joining a political party; get on a committee if you can.

Online. There are several websites, such as wealthymen. com, millionairematch.com, and others, where you can meet people. The goal here is to maximize your exposure and not to put all of your eggs in one basket. Most of these websites have small fees.

Local business seminars. A lot of men attend these events, and they are generally attended by the go-getter, motivated types. You might be one of the few women there. Fifty percent of them might be married, but get there a little early for the networking, and you might be staying a little later for a cocktail with a prospect.

Home Depot or Lowe's. These stores are a great place to meet men. Women tend to go to the decorative side of the store, but try the lumber and hardware sections. The men there will be attentive and want to help you. It's also a great place to meet your potential handyman who might not have a lot of cash but can save you some.

Car and Road Shows. Men love cars almost as much as they love women. This is a great place to meet men where there might not be many women except for the car show models.

Workplace. Get a job in a profession where the money is. If you are a secretary, look for a job at a law firm, an investment company, or doctor's office, etc. Whatever you can use to work your way into a good company might be worth it. You could go back to school to get a degree, or take a class in real estate, become an insurance broker, or just put yourself in a position close to money.

It is important to not always focus on money. You want a better quality of life, and money is necessary, but we don't want men to think that is all you are after. When you prospect, make sure you are taking into consideration that you have to like this guy. If you don't like him, it will definitely show. Find someone who is likeable.

Do not tell a lot of people your business. When you meet a girlfriend at the hotel, you do not have to tell her that you are scoping out guys who are likely to have cash. Tell her that you've always wanted to have a drink at a specific hotel to see what it is like or that you want to explore different lounges, settings, etc. After a few times, you might feel comfortable going out alone. I prefer going alone myself.

Do not have sex right away with any of your prospects. Do not get carried away if a guy is really sexy. You are a classy lady, so do not get drunk and lose control of yourself. Stay focused on why you are there.

Men—especially wealthy men—have many people saying yes to them. Saying no makes you stand out, and they want someone who is special, not someone who sleeps around. If you make them wait three to four months, you build intensity. I am sure you have had sex with a guy too fast, and he (and sometimes you have) lost interest. Make him wait a few months before you are intimate, and if he is into you, he should consider that very sexy; plus it forces him to get to know you better.

Once you get out there and start going to the places discussed earlier and start meeting the guys and began profiling, qualifying, and eliminating, you will look at the dating scene and men differently. Your needs and wants will be the emphasis, and they will change accordingly.

Most men respect you more when they buy you gifts as opposed to you asking them for money. But if they offer money, take it. Do not whine or cry when you express to them what you need or want. You'll find that some men like to be told what to do, and some will offer or just give you money every time they see you, but it's important that you not ask for money directly in the beginning unless they have offered it once already.

Make sure the timing is right when asking for something or telling a man what you want. Find some way to get over your fear or anxiety if that's an issue. A guy is just a person, and he has no problem asking you for something, so you should not have a problem asking him for anything as well. When you ask a man for something, it's all in your delivery. I cannot stress enough that you need to make sure you have read this man well and that he is compatible with your happies list. Make sure you have a sweet, confident tone, a smile on your face, and a sexy expression.

You can say almost anything to people if you say it correctly. Say things in a pleasant tone and manner; the reaction you get will be a lot different if you yell or are demanding. Overall, do not be afraid to ask a man for what you want; but be realistic, make sure that he is capable of providing it, and be sure that you have studied the guy well enough to try your luck.

If you aren't completely comfortable asking for things directly, practice using hints to warm yourself up for the kill. Although hints will work with some guys, do not make that a template for all guys. It's only practice to help you build your nerves. It's all about timing and giving him a facial expression and tone that he can't say no to.

Stay on the move and keep recruiting new guys; the more the better. Keep it casual and be uniquely refreshing and fun. Be the complete opposite of a nagging, clingy girlfriend. Show interest, don't be too available, have a life, have fun, and start feeling comfortable with getting what you want.

Chapter Three

How Do You Go About Getting It?

OK, let's say you have qualified a guy. You like him, you are hitting it off, and you have read the first two chapters, but you are still a little unsure how to proceed. Let's examine what you know and don't know to this point.

What you know so far:

1) The personality traits that guys like and look for in women

2) A few ideas about where to meet these guys

3) Which guys to avoid

4) How to listen and watch for voice tone and body language

5) How to open your mouth and ask for what you want in a sexy manner with a smile on your face

6) How to be yourself and not an actress

7) It's key to be fit, fabulous, and mentally healthy

What you might not know so far:

1) Some men will buy you things without you asking for them

2) Not every woman will be able to pull this off confidently

3) How to get to the next level of getting what you want

4) How to remain consistent once you start a relationship/friendship with these guys

5) How to specifically ask the right questions to get what you want

6) More in-depth techniques to get what you want

This is where you will need your self-confidence to really kick in. You have to carry yourself like you are the best thing since sliced bread, without any arrogance or conceit. The reason for this is so that when you're with your prospect or you are qualifying a prospect, you can make him believe this as well. If you doubt yourself, he will doubt you, too. When you exude happiness and confidence, it shows, and you glow. You have to be convinced and believe in yourself in order for anyone else to believe in you.

Make sure you do not get caught up in feeling bad by confusing getting what you want with something negative or going against your morals. You are not committing a crime or putting a gun to anyone's head. You can look at it like you are providing a service, if you will. This lucky guy will be happy to have such a wonderful person in his life who possesses your attributes and qualities.

One reason why many women are so emotional is because we were conditioned to think that way from the beginning. When an adult interacts and socializes with a female child, he or she might tell her she is pretty and speak to her in a soft, demure tone. Think back to when you were a little girl; did you play the game "house," where you were the mommy and you had a baby doll and a boy was your pretend husband? You probably insisted that your mother or father buy you a Ken doll for your Barbie, along with a Barbie Dream House with the pretty pink Barbie Corvette.

As an adolescent girl, did you ever fantasize about your future kids and what your husband would look like, along with that white picket fenced-in house? Surely you did at least one, if not all, of the things I described above when you were a young girl. I refer to this as the "Barbie World." This world is not real, but somehow as we get older, we still believe in this dream, and then we pass this fantasy on to our daughters and nieces.

On the other hand, young boys learn interaction in a rough, tough, macho style. Their play time with friends involves toy guns, blowing things up, and G.I. Joe figurines. Most men aren't as emotional as women, because they are conditioned to learn from an entirely different perspective from which they aren't taught to be emotional. Although they do know right from wrong, they might not feel as badly as women do when they do something hurtful.

Now, if you still believe in the Barbie World, by all means, I hope you find it and become very happy. I also hope that you have a wonderful life that many wish for and only a few get to experience. I am sure it does happen, but I am also convinced that the chances of the Barbie World happening is a pretty slim one.

Try to separate or shut off the emotional feelings and attachments that were forced upon you from the beginning of your childhood. Many men have been getting what they want from women without a second thought, returned phone call, an explanation, or a concern for a woman's feelings for years.

Men have had it way too easy with women, because many women in this world are living in a fantasy world, as if some romantic novel or movie is going to jump off the pages or off the screen. Prince Charming is not coming to save the day so that you can live happily ever after, because that is a fairy tale, not real life.

Wake up, ladies; real life is not a script where you already know the characters' lines. Creating a fantasy world within your imagination that is not relative with real-life experiences can be detrimental to your mental health. Please just enjoy the movie or novel, if you must fantasize for a moment, but then bounce back to reality as soon as possible. You are living real life; it is not lights, camera, and action!

Today you will create your own beliefs and morals for yourself.

It's time to change the way you think about dating men and getting what you want from them. Instead of thinking, "I wonder if he is going to like me," think, "I wonder if am I going to like him." Keep in mind that this is a numbers game, and you have to increase your odds.

Have you ever been approached by a guy who looks like a bum, and yet he still has the audacity to ask you for your name and number? Of course you have; we all have been appalled by this type of guy, and after we reject him, we usually go on our way.

The next time this happens, if you have a few extra minutes, pay attention. If this guy is loitering, leave and come back to the location, or go to a location nearby and watch him. I'll bet you a buck that he's trying his line on every woman and girl who comes across his path without any lack of confidence whatsoever. It's obvious that he is a loser, but it is also obvious that he is not taking rejection emotionally. How does he do that?

This guy knows the odds are against him, and that most women and girls will not entertain his advances, but this guy wants a female's phone number. He also knows if he persistently tries his line on as many women as possible, he is increasing his chances of a woman or girl giving him consideration. This is why getting what you want is a numbers game.

First, you will need to establish and keep your self-confidence high by developing a quick recovery process that'll prevent you from taking rejection personally or emotionally. When this system is fully developed, you should not feel discouraged when rejected, and you should easily dust yourself off and immediately bounce back with confidence.

Increasing your numbers means thinking somewhat like a man, by having tough skin and being able to think outside the box when you begin cutting through the red tape to get to your qualified prospects. Your biggest investment is you", so protect it. A healthy person knows that nobody knows you, or is going to love and take care of you better than you do, but there is nothing wrong with having men around to help you out along the way.

Lying is not a part of getting what you want from men. You will only tell them what you want them to know and what pertains to them. You should only spend time with a man whom you genuinely like something about. Don't ever consider yourself to be cheating on anyone, because your relationships should be casual, unless you have discussed exclusivity. If you do commit yourself to one of these gentlemen, own up to it, be honest with him, and treat him how you want to be treated.

Once you have your subject (qualified prospect) you should place him on a thirty-day trial to determine if he is really worth your time. During this period, you will take the time to get to know him and make him feel like he is very special and has your undivided attention. Also, at this stage, it is okay to tell him about your goals, dreams, and ambitions. Do not ask for money and gifts right away, as you might scare him away.

Be attentive, and become a great listener by practicing different listening exercises. This will help you if he notices that you remember things he's previously told you. When engaged in conversations, remember to incorporate the following:

—Flirty eye contact

—Lean in and touch his arm when you speak

—Display (light) affection,

—Always look fabulous

—Say his name a few times when you converse

—Always appear to be pleasant

—Smile

In conversation, you should pause and allow your guy to talk. He might provide some of the answers to your "happies" and "saddies" questions without you asking about them. He might even tell you some things he did for his exes, such as what he bought them and places they traveled. Feel free to ask him in a lightly joking tone, "What are we doing for my birthday?" This should work very well if your birthday is coming up soon, or ask something like, "When are you taking me on vacation?" whenever conversation about travel comes up.

Be mindful of how you ask for things. Always keep that sexy look, smile, and look your best at all times. If you are greedy, guys will pick up on that and might feel like you are never satisfied. You don't want them to think that they can't possibly do enough for you to be happy or that you don't appreciate the things they do for you. If a guy is giving you things, do not give him any reason to feel negatively about it.

Sometimes good things come fast. Just let them happen naturally and don't become a monster; stay grounded. Be sure to ask for what you want, but be realistic. If the guy just bought you a fifteen hundred dollar necklace, give him a break before you ask for another high-ticket item. Every now and then, if the guy is really good to you and if he tells you to get whatever you want, tell him, "All I want is you." He should feel really good about that, and give you so much more.

Do not change who you are. Women tend to start acting clingy or differently once they experience a man spoiling them. Be appreciative, and remain the woman you are, because that's who he is attracted to. You might have nicer things, but always remain the same person. Be humble and really appreciate the things you are receiving, and do not feel that gifts equal sex. A lot of times, the guy just wants you to be nice to him, and that's enough.

Of course, guys who spend money on you are probably sexually attracted to you, and more than likely, they want to have sex with you. If you are smart and play your cards right, you are spending time with someone whom you are at least mentally or physically attracted to, as well. On another note, you should not do anything with anyone until you are ready to do so.

It would be wise to not have sex within the initial thirty-day period. You must build intensity and mystery; it will drive them crazy. Do not tease or engage in sexually suggestive conversations. You are not a prostitute, so do not allow yourself to be treated like one. You are a wonderful woman who carries herself with dignity and deserves whatever she wants from a man whom you have a genuine interest in and/or attraction to.

You will know when it's an appropriate time to have sex with him. There isn't a time frame craved in stone to tell you when to have sex with a qualified prospect. I do recommend waiting a minimum of forty-five days or longer from the time you meet, depending on how consistently you are seeing him.

In some cases, the thirty-day rule might be thrown out the window if you find that after a couple of dates there isn't chemistry, or if you determine later that the guy falls into your "saddies" category, and you didn't pick up on that earlier.

See more than one guy at all times, and always be on the look out to increase your numbers by engaging in prospecting everywhere you go. Interview constantly, and ask for and always have a business card to give, because you might get lost in the cell-phone shuffle. If possible, create a hobby or entrepreneur business cards with your picture on them.

Create a database and place notes next to your qualifying prospects' names with their phone numbers, pertinent information about them, birthdays, favorite colors, where you met, how the date went, how many dates you've had, and any information or feedback that might be helpful to you with follow-ups. Keep track of which ones have reached the thirty-day trial period and when it's time to start asking for things that you want.

Be prepared for dates by referring to database notes before each and every date. The longer you see any particular guy, the more organized and familiar with his info you should be. In preparation for asking for what you want, it's okay to drop hints beforehand. When you drop hints, make sure they fit into the conversation. If you plan on going to school within a few months, start telling your prospects that you want to better yourself by learning something new, or that you want a career change, etc.

Before you start talking about school, the conversation should begin with a top news story about universities or a discussion about academics or self-enrichment, etc. It's important to start the conversation with an interesting topic to insure that your prospect is alert and that you have his attention. Keep it interesting and informative so that he hears you clearly, but don't overdo it.

Make sure you prep your prospect about a request at least two months in advance. Don't dwell on the subject, just touch on it a few times without becoming annoying. Ask him questions like "How do feel about _____?", and "What are your thoughts on _____?"

When you ask men for advice, they love it, so make them feel included in your decisions. A month before school starts, make sure you are in a situation where you are having a good time, and make sure the guy is giving you all the right signals that indicate he is really into you (phone calls, inviting you to dinner, events, always interested in seeing you again, consistency, etc.).

Once you are engaged in conversation and the moment seems right, smile and make eye contact. Ask in a sexy, sincere tone, "Do you think you can help me with school? It's starting next month." Pause and continue making eye contact with a soft smile and allow him to answer. Continue to smile with confidence as you wait for his response, and if he asks how much it is, make sure you know the answer, and tell him the truth.

Before you ask any prospect for financial help, it is imperative that you know enough about his finances to make sure he can easily afford the bill. If you have been doing everything described in this book so far, one of your qualified prospects might have already offered to pay for your classes when you told him that you were considering attending school. There are a few typical reasons why he would say no:

—He doesn't have the money

—You asked for it the wrong way

—Someone else is getting it.

If he says no, be cool and continue to be a lady, and politely ask why. He owes you an explanation, because you have been spending your quality time with him and telling him your personal goals and interests. If the answer sounds like BS, it probably is.

There's no need to become angry or upset. Do not feel compelled to end the evening abruptly; after all, the meal and drinks are still on him, plus you have other prospects you can approach.

If he calls you after he rejected your request, don't be rude; go ahead and answer his call. He might have good news. If he doesn't have a change of heart, politely tell him that you don't have time for him, because you are focusing on ideas on how to raise money for school. You just cannot fit him into your schedule.

Also, make sure that the last day he saw you was the day he turned you down. If he is truly interested in you and hasn't seen you in a while, by now he should miss spending time with you, and he might come around to offering you the money. Life is so unpredictable, and it is possible that the prospect who turned you down might change his mind. He might decide to give you what you want because of how you handled the situation by not displaying anger or hard feelings toward him.

On the other hand, if he doesn't offer you the money for school after your request, you shouldn't have to tell him not to call. It is likely that his calls will taper off if he doesn't plan on paying for your schooling. Unfortunately, some guys are cheap bastards in disguise. It will be your call to decide whether to speak to him again or to relegate him to the "friend file," which will be discussed later. Either way, you'll eliminate a guy while maintaining your lady status.

Take a moment and think about what you could have done differently and what you will do differently when you meet with your next prospect. Discuss with yourself what went wrong and how to prevent it from happening again. Please don't beat yourself up; simply reflect by playing everything back in your mind like a video recorder. In any case, be prepared to dust yourself off and move on to the next prospect with self-confidence.

Develop a system by creating a ritual or routine that will enable you to not take rejection personally. Treat profiling, dating, qualifying, and getting what you want as a business opportunity or venture.

Ask every guy in your database who has been around longer than the thirty-day trial period (and who you know can easily afford your wants) for the money or to purchase whatever your want is. While you are at it, complete a sweep or scan through all of the names in your database, and place all nonperforming prospects in a "dead file" that'll be discussed in chapter 4. If anyone has turned you down and has not bothered to call you back without any good explanation, delete him immediately.

For your protection, it is a good idea not to rush into sex with a qualified prospect until you know that he has your best interests in mind. Having sex with a guy who rejects your requests is not worth the emotional stress. When you do decide to have sex with a guy, make sure there is a plan behind it. Do it because you want to, or because he deserves it or has earned it.

Chapter Four

Learn the Man and What You Are Dealing With

Timing is everything. Let's say you meet a prospect with an extremely busy schedule that consist of previously planned vacations within days of you meeting him, or he has other obligations that prevent you from implementing your thirty-day plan. If he possesses all the qualities of being a great prospect, don't give up on him easily.

If your instincts tell you that this guy is genuinely interested, and that timing is the only factor that's preventing you from moving forward, you should create and place him in the not-yet file. Your not-yet file will consist of prospects who have current and future obligations that have caused difficulty in fairly placing them under the normal thirty-day evaluation.

These guys show interest in you by communicating and sincerely expressing how busy their lives and schedules are at the moment, with the intention of making time for you soon. Your job is to appear to be understanding and available in the future.

Review your notes from your not-yet file every month when you delete and add new prospects in your inventory. Working not-yet files works best when you have "low and/or slow" down time.

An example of a "low time" is when you have deleted all of your rejections from your inventory checklist and you haven't recruited or recouped new prospects because of your busy schedule or distractions. A slow time is when you just haven't had the time due to regrouping or restrategizing a new plan after a few rejections.

Although your not-yet file guys are out of sight, make sure they know they're not out of mind. Note all contact information, such as what you previously talked about, their interests, or anything else you feel is an important reminder, etc. Make regular, casual, consistent contact with your prospects, or occasionally email or call them and bring up things you previously talked about. They'll be impressed that you remembered your conversations with them. With the use of technology, you are still somewhat qualifying and excluding your prospects using a different approach.

Normally, it takes about thirty to forty-five days for a shift or change in their lifestyle before they will ask you out for lunch, dinner, or drinks. Grab a piece of paper and pencil and begin to draw a circle. Once you are halfway around the completion of the circle, stop. The complete circle is an example of how we live our lives.

When you stop at drawing half the circle, this side represents how you used to play tennis every Saturday with Suzy. Today you are on the other side of the circle, rollerblading with Becky instead of hanging out with Suzy, because you haven't heard from Suzy in a while. Once time passes, Suzy starts to call you again, or maybe you run into her somewhere and find yourself on the other side of the circle hanging out with Suzy again.

Let's go further. Suzy probably started missing out on tennis plans by telling you how busy she's been and that she wants to get together soon, so you gradually make your way back to the other side of the circle. At the same time, Becky is sure to be making her way to the other side of her circle of friends and activities as well. We all do it.

In retrospect, life is a circle, and in about thirty to forty-five days, these guys should be on the other side of the circle where you are, as long as you have made sure to keep in contact in order to remain in their minds.

Your not-yet file guys should receive photos and support from you when things are tough. You should assure them that things are going to get better, and that you can't wait to see them again.

When you meet them again, be at your best in every way. Have your best attitude, look your best, and be prepared to have a great time. Overall, think positively and have a bright outlook.

Live up to the hype that they might have created in their minds about you. Be bubbly, sexy, gorgeous, and carefree. Make them feel like seeing you is a need and a must. You want them to be so excited that they feel that meeting you today was better than what they remembered the last time they saw you.

If they really enjoy their time with you, they might make future plans with you, no matter how busy they are. Give them the most relaxing, fun, and drama-free time, and you will make their day and night. The goal is to make the right prospects happy, and in return they should want to keep you around and make you happy. Making you happy is getting what you want. Making them feel happy is one way for you to get it.

When you send your not-yet file photos, make sure they are sexy and do not cross the sleazy line. If you have to question it, don't send it. You want them to visualize you as a sexy, classy lady—not a sleazy one—so be careful of what you are conveying.

When you send them notes, emails, and text messages, make sure you keep them simple and personal at the same time, saying, for example, "I miss you. Give me a call when you have a moment, take care." Try to stay away from the typical, few-worded templates like, "Good morning, or "Thinking of you." This basically means or says nothing. After texting "Good morning" to someone, the proper response would be a simple "Good morning" back to you; typing "Thinking of you" might not even receive a response, and neither "Good morning" nor "Thinking of you" will stand out whatsoever.

The whole point is for you to stand out. You can make a better impression by texting, "Make your day go more smoothly by keeping me in mind," and attach a clear, cute headshot. Something like that will make a guy smile on a good or bad morning. Say what you mean, and try not to sound like everyone else. Don't think too hard and appear relaxed.

Avoid the following:

1) **Sounding conceited**—Be humble; be convinced of your worth but not conceited about it. Bragging and constantly complimenting your features and physical assets will only make you appear arrogant and cocky. It is not flattering.

2) **Being too seductive**—If you start off talking about sex and sending nude pictures, you are creating a situation where a man will only want to have sex with you and most likely will not respect you. Sexy, flirty, funny, and sweet are more like what you want to be in your prospects' eyes.

   Now, on the other hand, if you are engaging in a respectful sexual relationship that has been consistent for nine months or so, then your relationship would be steamier; just be careful when considering being more seductive. Never be over-the-top provocative to keep a guy interested.

3) **Being too cryptic**—Keep it simple and sexy; nothing too complicated is needed. Most people are not a fan of trying to figure out something that should be simple. You can be witty, but make sure that you aren't sending a Morse Code e-mail, note, or text. Your guy

shouldn't have to figure out what you are really trying to say; make sure he knows. Anything too subliminal can cause miscommunication, which goes hand in hand with misinformation. If you have a unique personality, make sure your guy knows you a little bit, so he knows where you are coming from.

4) **Pressing him for a date**—In the beginning, you are merely just getting to know him gently by touching bases and saying hi in order to keep yourself fresh in his mind. As time goes by, he will come around the circle, and you will meet again. In very rare cases, it might take longer than sixty days for your guy to be able to lighten his load, but if he has extreme qualifying potential, hang in there until you get your face time to seal the deal. You will have nothing to lose by waiting, because you will be busy increasing your numbers by prospecting and only following up during your low and slow times.

Keep working your inventory, update your notes to let him know that you remember things he's told you, keep in touch, wish him well, and offer him support. Don't pin him down for a time or a date. He will schedule a time for you, because you have been there for him and have continued to make an effort to maintain communication. If he doesn't make time for a date in a realistic amount of time, or if you begin to sense that he is not interested in you, move on immediately.

Make sure that all of the guys in your not-yet file are not rejects you just haven't deleted. Rejects are the guys who didn't give you what you wanted when you asked for it, or who haven't offered you anything of benefit within the thirty-day evaluation period time frame. If a guy continues to make lame excuses, lies, making and then not living up to his promises, or he just doesn't seem that interested in you, try your best to recognize these things right away, and once you do, don't waste any more of your valuable time. If more women would dump guys or set them straight before the BS increases, most men would be better people.

People can only do to you what you allow them to do to you. If you allow a guy to mistreat you, he will not respect you, and eventually you will feel played and used. When a man doesn't respect you, and he suspect that you are needy or clingy, he will take advantage. Keep the upper hand by staying in control of yourself and reviewing your notes to make sure you are on track.

Getting caught up with a guy who doesn't benefit you shouldn't be worth your spare time. Know when to say when and move on. Also, know when to take a break from prospecting when you are feeling a little burnt out. Regroup and reenergize yourself if you feel you are slipping into a negative outlook on prospecting due to a little failure. If you aren't thinking or feeling your best, set time aside and think about how to get it together quickly.

Do not chance going out on a date with a prospect when you aren't at your best. You are better off telling him that you are going on vacation and that you look forward to seeing him when you get back. Negative energy is ugly, and everyone in the room can feel it.

Too much of anything might not be good for you, and everyone needs a break once in a while. If you feel that you do need a break, take one. Taking a break every three months for up to two weeks is definitely recommended. Take a vacation with friends, hang out with family, or just roam around without eyeing anyone of the opposite sex (yeah, right). During this period, you might find yourself subconsciously prospecting prospects.

A lot of times, some of the most interesting prospects might come to you when you aren't looking or paying attention. Prospecting is a 24/7 job that you are not 100% consciously aware of. So know that it's OK to give your roaming mind and eyes a few weeks off from prospecting. Try not to be a prospect workaholic by thinking that you have to keep going when you are burnt out. If you push yourself to the point where you constantly think you might miss something good, you could be overdoing it.

If you have a couple of bad prospecting months or weeks in a row, take a break before you become self-destructive. After a little R & R, you can return to your regular routine. This is when you recharge your batteries and come back with a new plan of execution. When you return, begin your planning after reviewing your notes, revising all inventory and databases, and refreshing your prospecting files and techniques. Plunging back into the swing of things includes completing a self-examination without being too critical or hard on yourself.

Think of yourself as a big brand company. You are the board members, marketing department, CEO, etc., and take a look at how you can do things differently this quarter to increase business. Take a closer look at marketing. Did your profits plummet because of the places you met these guys? Did they have personality traits you should have avoided? Be sure to ask yourself questions and look at the facts only, and do not confuse yourself or create disillusioned reasons or discouragement. Your thoughts should be only of improvement and what's best for the company.

Taking a little longer than two weeks to get things back in perspective is OK, too. Nothing is going anywhere; it'll be there when you get back. You might want to be specific upon your return date with qualified prospects. Shoot a pleasant email with an attached smiling photo if you plan on being gone a little while longer. Keep it fresh and different, and make him anticipate your return.

When making your return from being burnt out, think about a highly qualified prospect who is showing or who has shown great interest by calling and spending time with you, passing the normal thirty-day evaluation with flying colors by being consistent and showing interest in your needs and your concerns. Focus on where you met this prospect and how you got so far with him, etc.

When conducting a thirty-day evaluation, I have said repeatedly to be yourself and not be an actress, but you need to also be an "adaptress."

An adaptress can adapt to every qualified prospect. This is why you should read, learn, and be informed on world news, trends, and other interesting topics. For example, if you have a prospect who is from another country, take the liberty to learn more than the usual topics and tidbits about that country.

Narrow down the particulars about the city or town he is from. Also, if he's a collector, learn about what he is collecting, or turn him on to this year's new "it" that collectors must have. Know your guys' interests, hobbies, career details, and what makes them happy and sad. Adapt to them based on what you hear, see, and learn from and about them.

Some men want to be told what to do, and some like submissive women. Adapting to your man without losing yourself is another form of getting what you want. It is not necessary to go along with anything way out of your character. If a guy starts making sexual conversation within the first couple of months, stop him. If he is vulgar and continues to repeat this behavior once you tell him to stop, this would qualify as one of the rare occasions when you might actually get up and leave a date without explanation.

Give a guy another chance after mentioning sex within the first couple of months only if he sincerely respects your wishes and doesn't attempt to initiate or hint at the conversation again.

Look out for, and don't fall for, lines such as, "We're both adults." You know that men are visual, so if you start talking about sex before a couple of months pass, he will be so consumed by it that he will bring it up every time. To get what you want, he needs to first think of you as a classy woman he wants to get to know.

During the first few months or longer, the sexual fantasies should stay in his head. Men will give you what you want just in the hopes of being intimate with you. Discussing sex too quickly with a prospect can lead to a disastrous distraction or interference from you getting what you want from a guy.

Unfortunately, most men are predictable and say some of the corniest lines that you have ever heard, over and over again. If a guy approaches and says, "How you doing today?" and you say, "Fine, thank you," and he replies with, "You sure are fine," you have just set yourself up to be turned off immediately by him. Be prepared to say something less predictable than "fine." Next time say you are fabulous instead of fine. Watch him light up like a light bulb. Now he is stimulated by your response and has to think of something more interesting to say in return.

If the guy appears interesting but happens to say something corny in response, it's okay to respond back with a clever twist in the same tone and manner he delivered. This can be an intriguingly good thing for him. Hopefully he doesn't say the same ole' thing back and can think out of the box in his next response.

If he does say the same lame thing, this could be a small indication that he might be set in his ways. As always, make eye contact and smile. If he isn't a potential prospect, it's okay to greet him and politely move along. As I discussed earlier, the way a man approaches you is likely the way he likes to be responded to, and most men aren't even aware of this fact.

In some cases, guys are corny, because that's all that has worked for them in the past, or they might be out of the loop. Hopefully, this encounter is taking place in an office environment, a network setting, or another social scene where you can talk and listen a little more before exchanging information and/or business cards. Either way, I am sure you'll raise a few eyebrows with the "fabulous" response.

Prospecting is an art, not a science, so you will win some and lose some. To get what you want from men, you have to have someone in your life to complement and add to what you already have.

To attract premium men, you must have goals, accomplishments, dreams, and aspirations. These make you stand out. Try not to allow yourself to get overly excited by what a guy can do for you; get excited by what the guy actually does for you.

Inventory is the major part of keeping up with your guys. Don't make it time consuming. With practice and trial and error, develop a quick, user-friendly organizing system. Complete a summarized note of your experiences and what you learn from the most valuable prospects. Place this summary in the very front of their file. Review the summaries when you are taking a quarterly regrouping break. Delete anyone whom you have discontinued.

Remember, your company improvements are based on facts and what you see in black and white, not on emotional delusions created in your mind. Documented profits and losses should be brief, detailed notes, not a dreadful task of reviewing drawn-out letters or stories. If you have to go through too much to get to the point, you will begin putting it off, procrastinating, or you will lose interest altogether.

Sharpen your prospecting skills with practice and by exercising what you have learned so far. Stay on top of where to meet more qualified guys like the ones you have been successful with.

For example, add new places to go and meet more prospects by learning what functions your qualified prospects like to attend or what activities they like to do.

Time wasting should not be permitted on your schedule, so don't pencil it in. The following should not be tolerable or acceptable:

- ☐ A prospect showing you disrespect
- ☐ A prospect giving you too many lame excuses
- ☐ Early sexual talk from a prospect

☐ A prospect not returning calls in a timely manner

☐ Showing interest in a prospect who's not that into you

If a guy becomes withdrawn because he knows you are about to ask him for money, he might not be generous or that into you. Pay attention to his body language.

Following the plan of asking for what you want at the right moment increases your chances of getting what you want.

Do not give up on a possible prospect who might be on the other side of the busy social circle. Your not-yet file prospects will come around eventually, as long as they show interest and you make an effort to communicate. Work these prospects when you are in a low or slow time to spark up your schedule.

Learn to adapt to any guy or situation without losing yourself. Learn to be an adaptress, not an actress, and do not confuse the two. Take everything you know so far, and like anything else, add your own personal touch to it. If you are a woman who has never been spoiled by a man, it's never too late to deserve it. If you are the type of woman who's always been nervous, shy, or uncomfortable around men, now is the time to get over it. There is no need to deny yourself respect with a little courtship and financial assistance.

Every woman's wants and needs will be different. Maybe you don't necessarily want money; maybe you just want a nice man to take you to dinner or buy you flowers. Whatever you want, you should have it. Now is a good time to get out there and start getting what you want. Practice makes perfect, so don't be discouraged. Before you know it, you'll have it, and what happens when we finally get what we want? Of course, we want more. Who knows, you might even want to get rid of some things that you have.

You might want to get rid of things you no longer have a desire or use for if it becomes a hassle. This is one of those situations where you evaluate if something is worth your time or not. If a prospect is giving you everything you want, but at the same time he is becoming a pain, you might want to get rid of him. You might have some unfinished business before you replace him.

I know you are wondering how can you get rid of things and still have it all. The amazing thing is that you can do it without any ill feelings. The main ingredient to having a positive outcome in this type of situation is to creatively think out everything and anything before you make sound decisions.

Chapter Five

How to Get Rid Of It And Still Have It All

OK, let's say you've had many successes and losses with your prospects. You have also received several things you wanted, and your guy is just smitten with you, but you aren't as smitten with him anymore.

You might come to a point in the relationship where you are losing interest and you are not sure what to do about it. This can happen for several reasons. Your guy might have become clingy and way too attached to you. He might say or do things that annoy you to the point you can't take it anymore. You might feel like one more second of him will make you scream.

You have a lot of things to take into consideration here, so take a moment and think about the energy you have put into acquiring this prospect. Start by asking yourself a few questions to sort out everything you're feeling.

For example, ask yourself: Am I annoyed to the point where I should really dump him right away? Can this situation be fixed? Is it him, or is it really me? What is it about this guy that is really bothering me?

Those are just starter questions to get your mind thinking before you react. Ask yourself a few questions to help prevent the mistake of finding out later that it probably wasn't all that bad, the problem could have been fixed, or that it was really you and not him at all. When you make a decision based on emotions only, you can end up apologizing for it later.

Guys might feel like you owe them something or they are entitled to something when they provide for you. It is essential for you to put a stop to this behavior as early as possible. Watch out for telltale signs by watching their reactions and responses after they buy you things. Are they acting a little differently?

Listen when they casually tell you about gifts they bought for previous girlfriends. Do they make negative remarks or comments about not getting anything in return? Do they say that she wasn't worth it? This is something you want to know, so creatively and briefly throw in related questions when you are prequalifying him, and if he speaks badly about every woman he's dated, he might be a walking problem.

Here are a few examples of unacceptable behavior and situations that might come up. These are also the kind of situations where you might feel that the qualified prospect's money and time are not worth the headache or aggravation. Think about your options and decide if you want to end the relationship.

He throws in your face the things he has done for you—There is nothing worse than thinking you have it made with a great guy who does all kinds of financial and wonderful things for you until the day he throws in your face all the things he's done. This is a real bummer and can make you want to kick this guy to the curb, but as always, think it through before you make a permanent move. For instance, try flipping the script.

Flipping the script is when turn around a situation that is not going your way. Once he starts throwing things in your face, he is probably feeling like he is not getting his way with you, or he might want attention and/or appreciation. When the guy starts whining about what he does for you, let him know he is appreciated by handwriting him a note and telling him how wonderful he is and how you are thankful for all of the things he has done for you. Go ahead and give him a hug and kiss to shut him up.

Your role in the relationship is to make the guy feel like he is getting what he wants in the relationship. Of course, it's on your terms only, even if the guy thinks it's the other way around. If you do not feel attracted to him, then he shouldn't be a qualified prospect in the first place. Keep in mind that you are his dream woman, so it's important for you to know how to play your role.

Sometimes all that these big babies need is a hug. Surprise him every now and then with a massage. If he is really good to you, surprise him by modeling lingerie for him. Visual stimulation is the best, but also try aural things, such as talking in a sexy voice and creating an alter ego to go along with the voice. Nicknames for you and your prospect are great, too.

When guys act out, most of the time it's for your attention. As women, we normally take this response from a man as a slap in the face. It's really not about what they have done, it's more about them feeling like you aren't showing them care, affection, appreciation or attention.

It's human to take some things for granted, and maybe you are. When a guy starts to complain that he does everything you want and you don't do anything in return, you should consider your behavior to see if he has a valid point. Be honest with yourself, and if you made any promises that you did not keep, it's up to you to fix the situation. If it's him, then you know your options.

You meet someone who has more to offer—This guy can offer you more, you like him better, and he is ready to give and is giving you more than the other guy. He also passed the thirty-day evaluation with flying colors. In other words, you have upgraded to a new vehicle that has the new-car scent and a smoother engine with quicker acceleration.

Slow down, sexy! You might not want to trade in your old vehicle just yet. Your "old car" has spent time, money, and energy on you, so he might not want to let you go so easily. He might want to put up a fight and step up his game.

His motivation is now his competition. If he has a competitive spirit (like most men do), let him know that another guy is interested in you and has been pursuing you with gifts. Do not give him all the details, just enough for him to raise an eyebrow and want to step it up and try harder. Don't be childish about it, but let him know in a loving, caring way that you wish he was the one doing those things for you.

Most men are competitive by nature and do not have to have an idea of what they are competing for, but if you have done everything right with your old car, he will give the new car a run for the honey. Tell the new car nothing about the old car, and it should stay that way until you have a new car to take his place.

If the old car doesn't step up, maybe he has a new car himself, or maybe he has lost interest in or outgrown your relationship. Make him sweat by proving that he will work hard to keep you. If he doesn't prove himself, he might not be a competitor, or you might find out the relationship is approaching its end. Know your guy's personality very well; this approach might not work on the sensitive or argumentative types. This approach should be used when the relationship has declined to where the guy has cut back on some things or you are fifty/fifty on keeping him or losing him.

He is less and less available and is doing less and less for you—This is obviously a problem. If this guy is married, he might be having a guilt trip, he might have a new friend in his life, he might honestly be super busy all the time now, or he feels something is wrong with you.

If you recognize a change in his behavior, unfortunately he might not tell you the truth if you ask him what's going on. A woman's intuition is a powerful tool. Do not let your ego or emotions prevent you from realizing that things are over between you and your prospect. Remain sweet, and just let him know that no matter what is going on with him, that you'll be available whenever he wants to talk.

Do not:

1) **Keep repeating yourself.** If you tell him once that you are available whenever he wants to talk, that's good enough. Bringing it up over and over again and asking him repeatedly if everything is okay isn't necessary.

2) **No whining.** I hear from men all the time that they cannot stand to hear a grown woman whine. Do not whine over the situation; it makes you look immature.

3) **Call more.** If you notice that a prospect's calls are becoming less frequent and he hasn't explained to you why you shouldn't be expecting to receive a call from him, just leave him one message in your usual pleasant tone. Let him know that you will not be calling again until you hear from him and that you hope all is well. Then hang up. It is more than obvious if he doesn't call you in a day (no more than two) that he has lost interest. If he doesn't explain that he's had a family crisis or a terrible car accident, etc., then for whatever reason, he might not be all that into you anymore.

If you do happen to hear from him later, don't appear to be angry or display any hurtful emotions. Try to jokingly make him feel bad. Continue to be fun and sexy, be yourself, and entertain his excuses. Most women would give him the third degree and would be emotionally upset and probably yell at him, but not you. You are going to set yourself apart by not showing any signs of being affected by his unreturned calls. He might never do that to you again, because he might feel like you are a really good friend because you weren't upset. From now on, he'll want to stay in touch, but now it's your game, on your terms. If this guy isn't giving you what you want, then don't waste your time.

4) **Allow a prospect who is giving little to pressure you for sex**—This is definitely not getting what you want. This idiot buys you a few groceries and thinks you are supposed to jump in bed with him. He is either very cheap in the first place, or somewhere along the line, he felt you conveyed that you were cheap.

That is not to say a prospect can't buy you something as nominal as groceries (especially if he takes you to the store; then he should definitely offer to pay). Nothing is too big or too small, as long as it's what you want. It's important not to make yourself known as the girl men can spend time with if they buy her a few groceries or fill up her gas tank. These should be some of those small things a man does for you; they are not a highlight. Your stock will plummet to a low-income housing project level in no time, if you think that you have accomplished something big while thinking on a level so minuscule. If you want upscale, you have to think upscale. You can't love yourself if you are subjecting yourself to settle for the lowest things on the totem pole. Remain full of pride and have dignity at all times.

5) **Have sex before a prospect starts doing anything for you**—This guy shouldn't make it past day fifteen. He's buys you dinner and drinks and has one thing on his mind. When you ask for something, he makes suggestions that he'll only provide for you if you give him sex first.

Remember, you are in a position where you are in charge of setting your own rules for yourself. Don't let this moron try to treat you like a prostitute; you have yahoo too much self-esteem for that. This is a great opportunity to flip the script on him. Treat him as a vehicle for you to conduct more prospecting at his expense. Since he is good for buying you food and drinks, take advantage of that.

If he wants to have sex with you before he spends the big bucks on you, you can keep this guy around as a dinner and drink date only, as long as he is respectful and kind to you. When you are out with him, discreetly eye the room and prospect for someone new. Lead this guy on with your sex appeal, and only meet him in public places when you have spare time. Friendly hugs and European cheek-to-cheek kisses will do.

After a few dates, you will roll this guy over like unused cellular minutes. As long as he is respectful, make him think you are hangout buddies who can chat about almost anything. After a while, you will be able to talk to guys around him and introduce him as a good friend. Here you are prospecting and eating and drinking for free, and this guy thinks you're buddies. It's pretty interesting how you can change a situation that you would normally walk away from to one that you can embrace.

Although this guy's game is pretty tired, you are only interested in playing if it's harmless. If he becomes irate when pressuring you for sex, do not tolerate him or his behavior. Dump him and cut him off immediately.

Overall, if you feel you have outgrown any guy you are seeing and want to go your own way, or feel like the money has slowed down, etc., take a few things into consideration. If this guy has provided for you by spending his money on you and helping you out in different ways, it's okay to remain friendly if that's what you want. You will be surprised how men will continue to provide for you if they feel you are a friend.

This kind of relationship adjustment happens in conventional and other types of relationships, so why wouldn't it happen here? Understand that some things just run their course, and it's a possibility that you might not be friends in the end.

There's no time to be bitter; you have to get out there and prospect. Take a moment to regroup if you suffered a loss. Surprisingly, your guy might heat up after missing you during the hiatus and begin making his moves toward renewal. It is possible that the "off" status might have been temporary or just due to a little misunderstanding.

After you let him know that you are there for him if he needs you, he might reach out and confide in you about what's going on or what has happened to or with him.

Some men will push you away when they are afraid of becoming too close or attached. Recognize this behavior by looking at the facts and allow them to speak for themselves.

If you continue to see a guy you have an issue with without thinking it over or discussing it with yourself or him, you are setting yourself up for aggravation. You will become even more frustrated with the guy over time, and that will lead to you taking it out on him. You might chance losing and contradicting everything you have worked so hard on, such as making him believe you are a fun-loving sweetheart.

By reviewing your notes thoroughly and playing back the time spent with your guy, you might see where things might have gone wrong. Write down on the left side of a piece of paper everything that is bothering you. Draw a line down the center of the page, and then write down possible solutions to your issues on the right side of the paper. Every solution you write down will brush away the negative energy you feel and the appearance of inconsistency that you might show. You are replacing inconsistency by creating ideas of how to diffuse issues unemotionally. Basically, by using the facts, you are getting to the point and the root of how to solve a problem.

As time goes by, you will learn about these guys, and you will know when and when not to dump them. If you question if a guy has been around long enough, or if you should touch base with him, don't feel obligated to continue communication if you thought it over thoroughly. You will know how you wish to proceed in this relationship from your previous experiences.

You know a time waster is not what you want. If a guy has given you a hard time and you haven't gotten anything small from him, then you already know nothing big is coming. The guy who has been genuinely nice to you, shows care, concern, and doesn't make you feel like you're pulling teeth to get what you want is the one that you want to stay around to be friendly with.

If a prospect has provided for you once, he will probably do so again. If he hasn't seen you in a while, make sure you are looking super hot. He will be invigorated all over again from the sight of you. This could lead to reactivating his file, but your new approach should be to see these guys at least once or twice a month. Do not settle for just seeing one guy at a time; as always, continue to prospect.

Even when you and your guys are just friends, still keep notes and keep it fresh. When this prospect is no longer a qualified prospect, this is where you create a new file, simply named the "friend file." Discard any new rejection files as usual. By now, you should have the prospect file, the qualified prospect file, the not-yet file, and the friend file. Any rejections should be deleted or trashed after a week or so of being in the dead file and the not-yet-discussed valuable file.

File Descriptions

Prospecting File—This file should consist of the guys whom you have met a few times and who have passed your happies/saddies test. They have what it takes to be a qualified prospect. You like what you see, and they say a lot of the right things. These guys haven't necessarily given you what you want yet, but in some cases, they already might have. This is during the thirty-day evaluation, which is the pre-qualifying preliminary interview for becoming a qualified prospect. Some of your prospects will be shifted to your not-yet file if applicable.

Qualified Prospect File—This is your guy. He has given you some things, if not all of the things, that you want, and he is into you. You have won him over with your style, class, and charm. Your qualified prospect is communicating with you on a regular basis and really wants to see you happy, because he adores you and knows you're worth it.

This guy has aced the thirty-day evaluation with flying colors. Nonetheless, qualified prospect status does change in some cases, and by now you should know how to determine status based on the prospect's behavior. Some of your previous qualified prospects will be shifted to your friend file.

Not-Yet File—If you meet a guy who cannot fairly complete the Thirty-day evaluation due to preplanned events or a crisis, he would go into this file. If he is a qualified prospect who suddenly became incredibly busy with a sincere explanation, he might fall into this file as well. Pretty much these guys have fallen off the radar, or time has gone by since you made one-on-one contact, but you still keep them in mind because they have potential and have continued to show interest with communication. You will have to follow your gut when deciding to terminate someone in this file.

Friend File—These are the guys whom you can get rid of and still have it all. They were lovers, providers, or guys who have been there to give you what you want, but things have since changed. You have outgrown him or he has outgrown you or interest levels have changed; either way, things are not the same, so he is now a friend, and you can still benefit from the new relationship. For this to work, you either had to be the one who broke it off, who distanced yourself from these men, or who flipped the script, not the other way around.

Try to avoid dumping any qualified prospects on bad terms, and make sure your mind is made up after thinking about it and thoroughly discussing it with yourself to ensure that whatever you decide is what you really want. Some of these guys might have been extremely great to you by blessing you with some wonderful things you've always wanted (and some might have been just okay). Either way, you will eventually feel like you want to move on because of several different reasons.

Dead File—If you are rejected by any prospect or qualified prospect (for the purpose of this book, the term prospect refers to a qualified prospect), complete your summary and deactivate his file immediately and place it in the dead file. This file is a temporary file that should only be open from ten to fifteen days. The purpose of this file is for the prospect to come around and offer you what you want after he rejected you. After the allowed time, terminate the prospect and delete his file for good.

Valuable File— Please see chapter 6 for more details.

Some of the strangest things can happen, and we never know what's around life's corner. The only thing we can do is to try our very best to be prepared for it.

Chapter Six

Moving On

Moving on is not so bad. It can be a good thing, because it's a part of growth and change. Your values might change, based on previous experiences. You'll think differently than you did before. You might have made changes in many aspects of your life, such as:

Evolving—You might have matured since you started your relationship with your friend or qualified prospect. By maturing, you think more and have a tendency to make better decisions, because you already know about consequences.

Prioritizing—Having a clearer picture of what you want and don't want will help you with reorganizing and re-categorizing your priorities. Your goals might be bigger or different from before, depending upon what you have already accomplished and what you want to achieve. Surely, you will have new goals, aspirations, and dreams that will replace the previous priorities.

Learning—When you move on, you open doors to a bigger and brighter future. Wisdom is what you hope to gain when reflecting on your life experiences. Learning from all your experiences should make you wiser. As you mature, you'll continue to develop into something more meaningful, and your goals and dreams will become more purposeful. The smaller things will count more, and you will probably do things you didn't really think about before; for example, volunteering or donating to a good cause, etc.

Other changes will occur as well, but the few things listed are designed to give you a head's up on the changes in life to come when moving on. You should become wiser in the future. If a qualified prospect hasn't provided for you financially or met any of your needs in a long time, it is time to start thinking about moving on. More than likely, if he isn't giving it to you, he is giving it to someone else. If it seems like there is nothing positive left, simply let it go and move on.

If you notice that you are down to a periodic email and a bunch of missed calls after having a wonderful, consistent relationship with a guy, you might be wasting your time today. There is no need to think about or worry about what he's doing for someone else, because apparently he is no longer doing it for you.

Pay attention to detail; if he hasn't met you for lunch, dinner, or drinks, and he's not taking you shopping or rarely answers your calls, it's a definite sign that he has or is beginning to move on himself. It's OK to think positively, but do not confuse positive thinking with denial. Denial will get you nowhere; do not hang on to someone who is showing signs of not wanting you.

Hopefully, you have followed the principle of not getting too emotionally attached. Your first experience with moving on might be the hardest, because you only know the traditional break-up methods. You might not have the unconventional experience to know how to detach yourself from your friend or qualified prospect. This could be extremely devastating, I'm sure, if this is the first man who has really spent money on you and invested his knowledge and time in you.

First, do not think conventional break-up. There are several steps to get over. Some steps might be new or familiar, but over time you will have to apply or add your own break-up remedies based on your personality and how you deal with problem-solving and personal issues. The result must be the same or quite parallel to a positive way of moving on.

Here are a few things to think about doing when moving on that might help you with the coping process.

Do not:

Think conventional relationship. In a conventional relationship, someone gets hurt, and you want to refrain from any deep feelings or emotional thoughts. This is no time for sadness or crying.

Think it over thoroughly more than once. Once you dissect your thoughts, think it over promptly. Then, decide on a plan for what you are going to do, do it, and let it go for good. Make a wise and smart decision, so that once you make up your mind what you are going to do, you stick to it. If you have trouble making decisions or getting constant thoughts out of your head, try putting your thoughts down on paper. Create a problem column on the left side of the paper, draw a line down the center of the paper, and create a solution column on the right side of the paper. This might help you to more clearly evaluate your problems.

Seek someone exactly the same or similar to your previous qualified prospect or friend. If you do this, you're still holding on to the past, and you have not completely or totally moved on. If you are not moving on, you are not moving forward, which means you are not moving toward your future.

Show signs of being affected. When people begin constantly asking if you are you okay, you will only look sadder, and it will become worse. People should not be asking you if something is bothering you or if you need to talk after a move-on. You should keep your business to yourself, and that goes for your body language, too. Chatting with friends will only create more sad feelings, and you will have to keep thinking about it, because you keep talking about it. A move-on should not affect your work or your time with family and friends. Once you decide what to do next, you should be completely over it. The end.

Don't be bitter. What's done is done, and one person shouldn't ruin it for everyone else. One sour apple should be just that one sour apple. When you move on, it's important to not be bitter, or it will affect you in the worst way. Your time is valuable and you should not have time to waste on that. Take a few weeks to regroup or start this book over if you are feeling bitter. You have to get it together, girlfriend.

Do:

Hang in there. This might be hard, but keep in mind that this is business, and in business you have career highs and lows. It's not all win-win, but keep your head up and remain optimistic.

Close or delete your previous qualified prospect or friends file. Once it's over, there is no reason to keep his file. Scan through it one final time in case you missed anything worth keeping. Take a few notes in your valuable file. This is a notebook that you will have tabs in. The tabs will have valuable lessons learned or situations where you did well or things you would have done differently.

Customize your tabs by deciding what information is most valuable to you. Refer back to your notes for future reference when necessary. Once you gather the information that you feel is valuable enough to keep in mind in the future (which can also come from your summaries), then close it out for good. (The valuable file can also work great when rolling your qualified prospect to a friend file). When closing out any file, remember the dead file option.

Focus on current prospects. Continuously prospect, prospect, prospect, and qualify and eliminate as normal. No matter whom you are seeing, you should always be playing your numbers.

Continue your life as normal. Forget about all the words you hear in love songs. You can live and breathe without him; trust me, there are more out there where he came from, and they are dying to meet you. Sometimes you have to allow some good things to come to an end in order to allow great ones to begin.

Always regroup if necessary. Not every break-up should require this, but in some cases, it might be very necessary to go on a getaway or to use whatever regrouping technique that works for you. Take care of yourself and get back into the game.

Protect your self-esteem. Depression, sadness, and anger are negative emotions that you do not need in your life. Remember and refer back to the routines and rituals discussed earlier, and make sure you are following a formula in order to keep yourself healthy.

Stay busy. With every loss, self-examination should be automatic. Take a few moments and learn something new about yourself during this process. Develop or recognize a new happie or saddie that you might want in or out in your life, then let the activities begin.

Like everything else, you will be able to add to this list and create your own dos and don'ts where they will come naturally. With practice, you will become a professional. Your thoughts should be more about your experiences and about moving on to tomorrow without leaving a bad taste in your mouth today. Do not be negatively affected by moving on. Look at this as a positive, reflective time where you have a great opportunity to spend quality time with yourself.

Before letting one of your friends or previously qualified prospects go, ask yourself what you have learned from the experience. What have you learned from him? Recognize changes in everyone and everything often, not only when things are falling apart. Try not to let anything slide, if possible.

To move on successfully, you must be fully aware of the mental part of moving on and the thinking process that goes along with it. Your way of thinking will be an advantage over most women's thinking. Your ability to think clearly and not emotionally will become second nature over time.

When coping, do not display sad body language. Behave normally, keep working out and solving your problems and/or issues, and move on. Consider completing a wonderful exercise called centering. Centering is where you create body and mind balance by tapping into your spiritually connected side.

Start doing activities that mean something to you or that do positive things for you. Centering and coping after a relationship is similar to reconnecting to the Internet after a lost wireless signal. You are the computer, and the Web is your channel. You search within your channel to find things that pertain to you and your focal interest. By developing a routine of activities to help you refresh and repair your wireless router connection, you have already begun the process of centering yourself.

Your routines should relax you, create awareness, and sometimes distract you into thinking about other issues. You will do some of your best thinking ever when you take time for yourself as you center and revive. Try such activities as:

A day at the spa—Having a massage, facial, and other treatments will take the stress away and help you form happy thoughts.

Meditation—Meditation is the epitome of all centering. Try yoga, prayer, chanting, or whatever meditations you've learned or plan on discovering that make sense to you.

Hobbies—Try one of your favorite hobbies that you haven't done in a while, or explore something new or extreme. Google things to do in your city.

Get a makeover—A fresh start can also lead to a new look and/ or new clothes. Try a new nail color or design. Tell your stylist to give you a new hairstyle or check out a few hair magazines and see what styles you like. Department store makeup counters will do your makeup for free if you call and make an appointment.

Shopping—This is a woman's therapy, and if you can afford it, definitely do it. Go to a boutique, do some discount shopping, or catch a super sale. Once you have your new hairdo, fresh nails, and new makeup, all you are missing is your new, sexy dress.

Take a class—Why not learn something new? Learn Spanish or learn how to sew or rock climb. Get the picture? Experiment with something new or different that you always wanted to do.

Cook—I do some of my best thinking when I cook. Cooking is also relaxing, and if you are like me and enjoy gourmet cuisine, you will probably have cookbooks to follow. Invite a small group over and have them bring the wine.

Create your own—No matter what I suggest, you still have to come up with your own thoughts and ways of doing things. No one should know you better than you know yourself, so you should know what works for you. Be creative, innovative, or simple.

If your friend or previously qualified prospect wants to move on because of something you did or said, take it with a grain of salt. Go ahead and explain yourself after thinking the incident through without bias. Be apologetic if you hurt his feelings or if you discover you were wrong. Be a woman of your word and follow through, even if you really don't feel like it, unless you have a valid reason that keeps you from doing so.

Let him know sincerely that you did not intend to offend him or hurt his feelings. Even if that's not the case, you should apologize anyway and attract a bee to your honey; you might be rewarded later. If you explained yourself sincerely, and if he doesn't forgive you, simply move on.

You cannot change anything that has already happened. You took the initiative to offer a sincere apology. He left you with no choice but to accept it and learn from it. If you blew it with a great prospect because he doesn't find it in his heart to forgive you, make sure he isn't flipping the script with reverse psychology.

If your qualified prospect or friend says something like, "I'll forgive you if you make it up to me," pay attention to the words that come next. Listen to his tone and watch his body language, and if he says he wants you to do something sexual or something that you wouldn't normally do, he is playing the "guilt game."

The guilt game is where he will talk you into doing things to his advantage or gain at the expense of making you feel guilty for whatever you did or said; the key words being "to his advantage."

Although moving on is about you, you still continue to think about the other person. Make sure you do not fondly reminisce when rethinking and reenacting the events and situations that have previously occurred. If you find yourself slipping, immediately take yourself out of the equation and focus on the events only.

The difference between reminiscing and self-examination is that self-examination is about self, and reminiscing is something that people in conventional relationships do when they think about the other person in the relationship. When people in conventional relationships break up, they tend to focus on the other person, the things that they've done together, and the times that they've shared.

Since you have already thought over the situation initially and talked to him about it and pretty much moved on from it, there is no need to think about him or his feelings any longer. After documenting your notes, your thoughts should be about what you have gained, what you will do differently next time, and what you have learned and how to apply it in your prospecting.

Every situation will be different when you break it off with a friend or previously qualified prospect. You must be honest and straight up about it. No impulsive decisions should be made. It is hard for me to tell you exactly what to say, because every situation will be different, but I can tell you that it's best to be honest (about your feelings toward him; do not display personal business), straight up, and clear.

Do not talk in between the lines, unless that's the way your friend or prospect generally communicates and processes information. Watch how you say things and your body language, and make sure they are saying the same thing. Don't be wishy-washy, because you will appear to be a person who doesn't say what she means or means what she says.

You have to be taken seriously by your prospect(s) in order for him (them) to possibly stay in your corner when you move on. If he can say that you have always been honest with him, you might have a chance of him taking you seriously as a friend because of your honesty.

Your friend or previously qualified prospect needs to believe that you have been honest and loyal to him if you plan to contact him in the future. He might think of your honesty after your break up, and this makes it easier if you contact him again if you want something.

Being honest with your friends and prospects is the foundation of gaining these guys' trust. As you approach moving on, you want them to keep positive thoughts of you, because you might need them again. This predicament is a little different from the typical friend file guy that you have when moving on and having it all, because you actually remove yourself from his life but keep him in your corner pocket for future events. After you break it off with this friend or prospect, you remain in contact with an email or phone call once or twice a year (birthdays, etc.) to say hi and to fill him in on your goals, etc., to make sure he will still have your back when necessary.

Wait a few months before contacting these guys after a break-up. This will give them time to miss you. It is okay for them to have conventional feelings for you, but not the other way around. When you do decide to make contact, be polite and ask superficial questions like "How have you been," etc. At this point, it's almost like profiling, similar to what you did when you were getting to know him.

Annually or biannually, send him a brief email, text, or call telling him something that he might be interested in knowing, or ask him something that you think he would be surprised that you remembered, etc. Be careful to keep your distance, and keep it simple and real by being yourself and cordial. When you feel the time is right, ask him for something or suggest meeting for dinner or coffee, etc.

Talk to him like an old friend or buddy when you meet with him, and let him know what you have been up to. As usual, make sure you are looking like your sexy, gorgeous self. Since this guy has already provided for you previously, it should be a breeze to get what you want from him unless he has a grudge. Start off somewhere in the middle. Don't ask for big-ticket items right away, unless he offers. You really want him to know you are sincere, so don't make him feel used. Try to meet him no more than once or twice a year.

You will be surprised by how most men will still be willing to give you what you want even if you have broken it off with them. Just by remembering a few small things, you now have a history that has evolved. This might not work with every friend or previously qualified prospect, but it will work with some of them. In some cases, you will find that if you break it off with a guy, he might not want to be bothered with friendship, but the others will make up for him.

The friend-file guys are those guys who you are simply warming back up to being qualified because of a light fizzle or you are just hanging out with for dinner, drinks, and prospecting. With "moving-on" friends, you actually break it off, but you still see the potential to receive what you want from them.

In the end, you will appreciate and learn from all your successes with friends and previously qualified prospects. The rewards will be plentiful when you master how to get rid of it all and still have it all. When moving on, you will see yourself moving up.

This purpose of this book is to get you to think about yourself, what you want, and teach you techniques on how to go about getting it. Most women put their men before themselves and end up losing themselves in the process. If you take away a woman's emotional side when she is dealing with a man, she will have much more power and control over that man. The power would come from her being able to think rationally without her head being clouded with emotions.

Instead of fantasizing about the picket fence and the big yard for the kids to play in, you have to think outside of the box. Times have changed drastically and will continue to change, and women need to stay ahead of the game or they will simply get played.

Chapter Seven

Success

When I began arranging this book, my goal was to provide a step-by-step guide to keep the reader's interest. I find that a lot of self-help and information books drag on interminably, and before you know it, you've lost interest before getting halfway through the book.

In the first few chapters, you learn skills and things about yourself that you can apply to everyday life immediately. Once you are ready to move on to the next level of learning, all you have to do is go to the next chapter. Instead of flipping from page to page, trying to get to the point or getting bored with the book altogether, you are excited and look forward to finding out what's next. Although you'll find that some information in this book is common sense and reinforced reminders, you can still learn something new.

Your views on men, dating, and most importantly, getting what you want without letting emotions get the best of you, will settle in. Women have been accepting the worst from men for centuries, and in the end women have cried the same blues over and over again.

Getting what you want isn't just about getting money or gifts from men; it should be about a lifestyle. It's also about self-worth, gaining knowledge, and not allowing emotions to take over. Allowing your emotions to influence your decisions can bring negative effects such as insecurities, self-esteem issues, and any other negative issues that women go through when a man deceives them, lies to them, or cheats on them.

The whole idea is to protect yourself from the repercussions of conventional relationship drama that we all have endured. Everyone will not agree with your new lifestyle, but I'm sure many of them will agree that a lot of people do not have relationships these days; many of them are just having sex. The difference between you and them is that you are creating an image in exchange for getting what you want without disrespecting yourself.

Many women who engage in casual sex fantasize about the possibility of becoming the guy's girlfriend. Some women do it because of loneliness or promiscuity, but it always boggles my mind that so many women are willing to go home with or take home a guy just for sex. A lot of guys can easily sleep with different women every night and brag about it, but when women sleep around, they will keep it to themselves unless they're getting something more out of it, such as money or gifts.

Women should want and expect a lot more from men, and if they'd band together and demand it, perhaps men wouldn't treat them badly. Understand that you can't take men too seriously. Many of them lie to get what they want, so protect yourself by not placing any of them on a pedestal. Finances, knowledge, a good time, travel, fine dining, or whatever else you have on your list of wants are the things you want from these guys. Sex should come later down the line, and it shouldn't be a priority.

The end result of many conventional relationships is sadness. Once he starts lying to you or trying to convince you that you are the only one, why should that matter to you if you are getting what you want? All you have to decide is where to place his file and what other qualified prospect or friend to attend to next.

Controlling your emotions will take time and practice, because you have been trained all of your life to do the opposite. Think back to a time where you were so emotional that you reacted in a way that you later regretted. When confronting an issue, you have a better chance of responding sensibly when you remove emotional overtones.

Once you have complete control of your emotions, you'll have control over your life. You'll feel a lot happier and healthier and be ready to achieve whatever you want to accomplish in life. Depression or negative mental states can result from being an emotional wreck and hinder your ability to feel free.

There are several things you will learn on your own, because every situation will be different. You are human, so you will make some mistakes and think that some guys are worthy, only to find out later that they aren't. You might even have sex with a guy because he is at the right place at the right time. Part of controlling your emotions is controlling your sexual urges. Develop a way to counter sexual urges when you aren't sexually involved with a qualified prospect.

Controlling sexual urges is mind over matter, so do your best to make the right decisions. Subjecting yourself to a booty call should not be acceptable ever. Always get something out of the situation, even if you have already decided that you want to have sex with a guy. It can be as simple as having a guy take you to an expensive dinner or on a shopping spree; just be sure to get something more than sex.

Getting what you want from men does work better when you make the guy wait for sex. Do your best not to have sex with a prospect right away. Be mindful that if you have random sex with a prospect or sex within the thirty-day evaluation period, you might not get what you want from him, because he has already gotten what he wants from you. Although it might be challenging, do not beat yourself up if you have a few slip-ups. Dust yourself off, move on gracefully, and remind yourself that romance without finance is nonsense.

It wouldn't be true or fair for me to say that every single move I've discussed with you will work on every single man you come across. Some men have been played by women, and they might think you are trying to manipulate them or playing similar games that they have previously experienced. Players or guys who are only out for one thing might fall for you, because you aren't the everyday, average, or clingy woman. Men will be drawn to you because of your uniqueness.

Any man who feels that every woman is out to put something over on him is another example of a walking problem. If you don't avoid guys with similar issues, you will soon be babysitting their egos. Whenever you feel that you are putting too much work into a prospect, you probably are. Desperation and frustration shouldn't be words that describe maintaining an unconventional relationship, because those aren't the things you want. Nonetheless, in any situation with any prospect, remember that timing is essential.

Social settings, such as lounges or nightclubs, are the most common places to get lucky, if you go to the right places at the right times. Unfortunately, because of imposters, these aren't the best places to meet men on the weekends. You will come across a lot more quantity than quality when going out on the weekends.

Men with money tend to go home early. When going out with the intention to profile, attend an upscale happy hour or an upscale lounge if you want to meet better quality men. If you are into nightclubs, it's best to attend them when going to special events or during weekdays.

Attend VIP birthday parties for successful people and catered private/special events. More than likely, your successful friends will invite their more successful friends, and you'll profile and make new friends all evening. Research expensive brands (such as liquor brands, luxury cars, etc.) that promote and sponsor high-end events and sign up on their websites to receive invites to their private events. It makes more sense to go out with a plan instead of just hanging out.

Some guys will have a straight-up approach and will appreciate you being straightforward about how you want to be treated by a man without sugarcoating it. On the other hand, some men want you to be more subtle, and it is your job when profiling to know this before a man makes the prospect status.

As discussed earlier, when you listen to men and watch them, they will indirectly give you the basics on who they are and what they want. The way they approach you is the way they like to be approached. The way he touches and kisses you is the same way he likes to be touched and kissed back.

If you find that overall you like everything about a prospect except for a few small issues, you might still be able to find a use for him by suggesting corrective techniques. Never feel shy or overwhelmed when correcting any prospect's minor flaws, especially when you have practically considered a guy a qualified prospect. Make everything appear comfortable and easy. Your vibe should be natural, like you are letting everything roll into place. You will definitely come across some minor nuisances when prospecting, but stay mindful about your purpose.

You aren't looking for perfection or Mr. Right; it's more like Mr. Give Me What I Want or Mr. Right Now. If your qualified prospect has a great personality and is giving you everything you want, then his looks shouldn't be the main thing you focus on. A good-bye kiss from the most unattractive man would be very hard to digest, so handsome men should be very welcomed, but don't cancel someone out because he isn't a Brad Pitt or Boris Kodjoe.

In conventional relationships, we look for a tall, dark, and handsome knight to sweep us away into the faded darkness, but what do you do when the credits start to roll and the movie is over? The dream man, as far as a qualified prospect goes, is not necessarily the most handsome guy in the room. He is the one who meets your happies list. If your qualified prospect is caring, considerate, and gives you what you want, who cares that he isn't 6'2"?

In some cases, you might have to encourage a slightly overweight prospect to lose a few pounds. If he helps you out and that's your only issue, why not help him out, especially if he is serious and willing to get in shape. He could possibly be a qualified prospect. Make sure you are getting what you want before you go out on a limb for any prospect. If a guy isn't willing to make a positive change, throw him back on the bus and continue prospecting.

When profiling, make sure you have properly determined your guy's questioning style and have built a strong rapport before you ask specific happy or saddie questions. You might want to hold back some questions until your second date. If you sense apprehension, nervousness, or discomfort over the phone or during the first encounter while asking questions, wait until you are face to face again to ask your remaining qualifying questions. Remember not to ask typical questions that he has heard so many times.

Dinner and meetings with your prospects should include conversations about your goals, dreams, current events, etc.

Remember, most men want to feel needed, and it is very sexy for a woman to have a good head on her shoulders. A man can appreciate helping a woman who wants to help herself.

Do your very best to be observant when your guy is telling you what he wants from you and who he is. The things he tells you and the way he touches you say a lot. By gathering this information, you are halfway to getting what you want if you apply everything you have learned correctly.

For example, let's say you are meeting a prospect for dinner, and over conversation he mentions that he is very giving and generous to people who are there for him when he needs them. Instead of thinking, "That's impossible, no one can be that available," you can work this situation by saying in a cute, sexy voice,

"You should be generous to me, sweetie, because I am here when you need me right now." He'll get it if after you say it, you make eye contact, lean in, smile, and let out a small (real) laugh.

Most women I know want to be married, want to feel wanted, desired, and cared for. Do you really want to live with a guy, do his laundry, and cook his dinner because you are so-called "in love" with him? On Christmas, if you had to choose, would you really want gifts or the guy? This book is for those who want the gifts.

Being in love is a state of mind, and if that's what you want, by all means go for it, but if it isn't, then why bother with it? If a situation smells like crap, under normal circumstances, it's probably crap. Never be blinded by BS, and do not allow yourself to be plagued with denial. Be selective with these guys; some of them are really deceptive. Do not judge them by their attire, cars, or looks alone. In this day and age, men's clothes are not as expensive as you think. Although it might be difficult to remove emotion from any relationship, know that practice makes perfect. When you are too emotional, you create drama, and with drama, there's always conflict with communication. Everyone knows an emotional person whom they do not feel comfortable sharing certain things with because the person might not be able to handle it without drama. Don't be that person.

Be smart, pay attention, and remember to always take a few moments at least once a week for self-examination. Clear your mind and take a deep breath before you begin fine-tuning and reorganizing your inventory. Stay organized the best way you can, by keeping your prospect files and prospect notes logged correctly and updated regularly. There is no need to become a stickler, but you need to remain on top of things.

Stand in front of a mirror and smile at yourself, then make different expressions with your face. The purpose of this is to have an idea of what you look like when you make certain faces and to make sure you are conveying the look you intend to. Make sure you can relate your facial expressions to your feelings. Take another look in the mirror and think about a time when you felt like a sexy diva or a sex kitten, and watch how your face lights up from within with crazy sex appeal.

Look at yourself one more time and take notice of the changes you've made since obtaining this book. You have learned some valuable tips and techniques that I have personally used in my everyday life, and they have worked quite well for me. If you apply them correctly, they can work for you. Be proud of yourself for beginning your journey to success by deciding to change what you have been conditioned to think your entire life.

The true success here comes from you learning who you are and knowing what you want. Below are some of the most important guidelines you must follow in order to complete your successful journey to getting what you want from men:

*Be at peace with yourself

*Know yourself

*Control your emotions

*Prospect daily

*Use all the tips from this book

*Create some of your own techniques

*Never be afraid to ask for what you want

Please send me emails about your endeavors, successes, and any questions you might have at getwhatyoureallywantfrommen@live.com. Also, be on the lookout for more books to come, as well as "Getting What You Want" seminars and workshops. Thank you for reading my book, and I wish you the best in getting what you really want from men.